Copyright © 2022 Jessica Brittani

All rights reserved. No part of this book may be reproduced, distributed, or transmitted in any form or by any means, including photocopying, recording, or other electronic or mechanical methods, without written permission of the author. The only exception is by a reviewer, who may quote short excerpts in a review. For permission requests, email the publisher directly, addressed "Attention: Permissions Coordinator," at jessica@calmandcolorful.com.

The information contained in this book is intended to be educational and not for diagnosis, prescription or treatment of any health disorders. This information should not replace consultation with a competent healthcare professional. The content of this book is intended to be used as an adjunct to a rational or responsible program. The author and publisher are in no way liable for any misuse of the material.

For information about special discounts for bulk purchase, please contact the author at (805) 618-2526 or jessica@calmandcolorful.com.

Graphic and Book Design: Gemma Dunne—gemmadigitalart@outlook.com

Cover Layout Design: Fresh Design

ISBN: 9781732183117

*I dedicate this book to my cousin
Rachel Elizabeth*

This book belongs to:

_____

Table of Contents

1. I am safe
2. I am healthy
3. I am loved
4. I am wise
5. I am strong
6. I am capable
7. I am worthy
8. I am enough
9. I am heard
10. I am balanced
11. I am focused
12. I am positive
13. I am generous
14. I am secure
15. I am grateful
16. I am confident
17. I am courageous
18. I am powerful
19. I am patient
20. I am creative
21. I am talented
22. I am intelligent
23. I am free
24. I am grounded
25. I am peaceful
26. I am protected
27. I am brave
28. I am unique
29. I am unstoppable

Positive affirmations are statements we make to ourselves that communicate positive messages to create the life we want. They help us program our brain that creates positive outcomes which step into being the person who we want to be.

Benefits of Positive Affirmations:

→ Uplifts your mood

→ Motivates you to step into self growth

→ Changes your negative thought patterns into positive thought patterns

→ Improves self esteem, motivation, and productivity

→ Helps with anxiety and success

→ Supports you to stand in your power

→ Allows you to become more aware of your daily thoughts, words, and self-talk

Tips & Tricks:

→ Evoke positive feelings as you read or say your affirmations

→ Start slow

→ Practice every day for 28 days to build a habit

→ Use empowerment poses while saying affirmations

→ Sometimes it feels silly saying some affirmations, but the more you practice them the more comfortable you will feel saying them

→ Combine affirmations with action– affirmations are meant to be a step towards making change

→ Be patient & consistent

→ If the affirmation doesn't make you feel incredible, add words like *"becoming"* i.e. "I am *becoming* confident" to make it feel more realistic and relatable

You will see this page next to each Affirmation image.

Below, it explains the purpose of this page and how to use it.

Positive Affirmation

Self Assessment: Notice how you feel before practicing this affirmation. Recognizing how you feel in this moment will help you stand in your power. You have control of how you feel, which is why it is important to recognize your feelings.

What is your self battery level before practicing?

Before exercise:

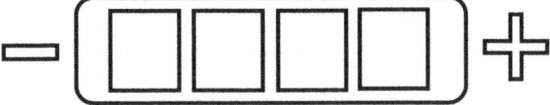

Empowerment Pose: Standing in an empowerment pose helps you proactively influence your outcome of creating the feeling of this affirmation. Anchor in your affirmation with an empowerment pose.

Intentional Emotion: Write the emotion you want to bring into the exercise in this space.

Scribe: Writing is so important and helps connect pathways in our brain quicker than just saying things out loud. Write affirmation in this space.

Repeat Affirmation Aloud: Use this space to tally how many times you repeat the affirmation.

Reflection: Notice how you feel after practicing this affirmation. Where you are able to identify your feelings, the better you are able to understand yourself.

What is your battery level after practicing?

After exercise:

I am safe

Self Assessment: What is your self battery level before practicing?

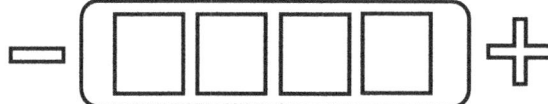

Empowerment Pose: Compassion Pose
Stand in this empowerment pose for two minutes while repeating this affirmation.

Intentional Emotion: Write the emotion(s) you want to bring into the exercise in this space: _____
_____

Scribe: Write affirmation in this space: _____
_____

Repeat Affirmation Aloud: Use this space to tally how many times you repeat the affirmation:

○○○○○○○○○○○○○○○○○○○○○○○○

Reflection: What is your self battery level after practicing?

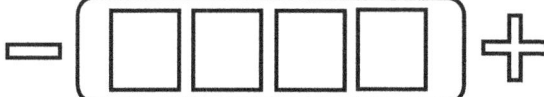

Visualization helps to deepen positive affirmations. Helping you step into the best you that you can be! Can you draw out your visualization below?

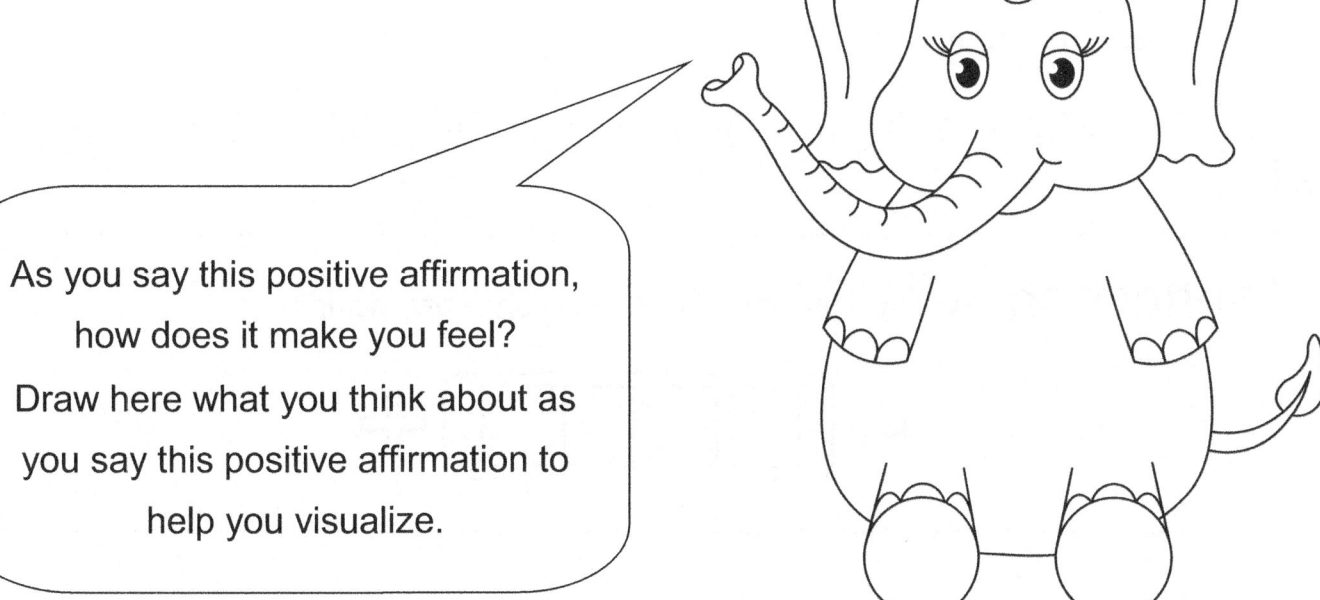

I am healthy

Self Assessment: What is your self battery level before practicing?

− ▯▯▯▯ +

Empowerment Pose: Worthy Pose
Stand in this empowerment pose for two minutes while repeating this affirmation.

Intentional Emotion: Write the emotion(s) you want to bring into the exercise in this space: _____
_____

Scribe: Write affirmation in this space: _____
_____

Repeat Affirmation Aloud: Use this space to tally how many times you repeat the affirmation:

○○○○○○○○○○○○○○○○○○○○○○○○

Reflection: What is your self battery level after practicing?

− ▯▯▯▯ +

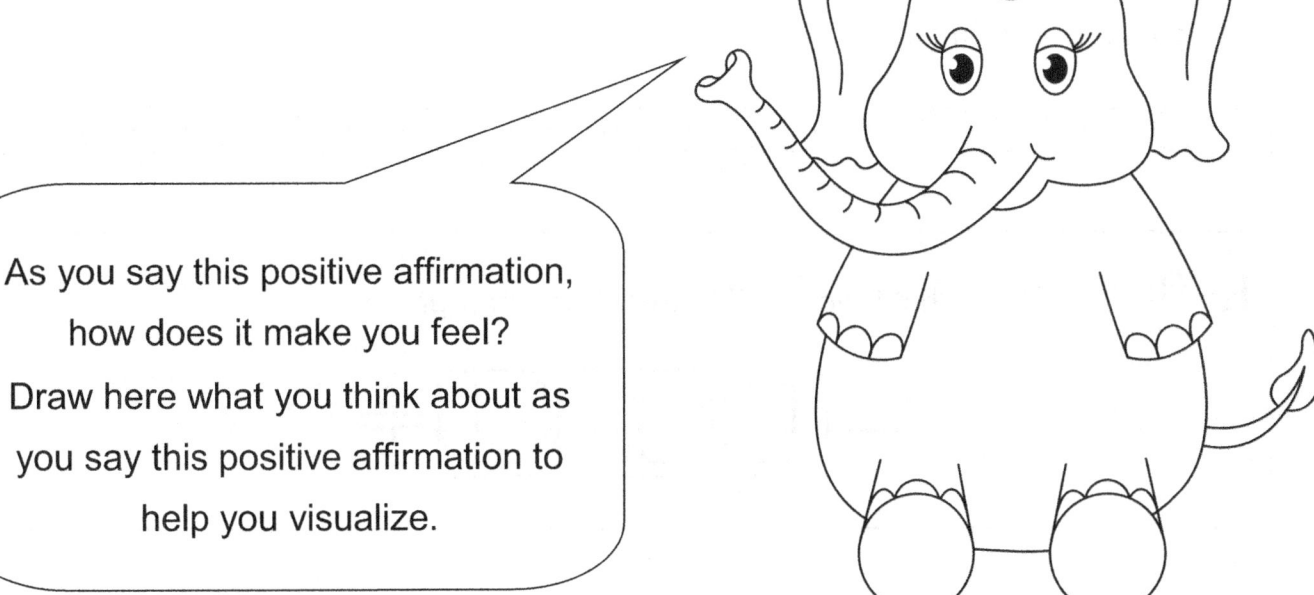

I am loved

Self Assessment: What is your self battery level before practicing?

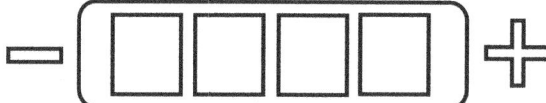

Empowerment Pose: Embrace Pose
Stand in this empowerment pose for two minutes while repeating this affirmation.

Intentional Emotion: Write the emotion(s) you want to bring into the exercise in this space: _____
_____

Scribe: Write affirmation in this space: _____
_____

Repeat Affirmation Aloud: Use this space to tally how many times you repeat the affirmation:

○○○○○○○○○○○○○○○○○○○○○○○○

Reflection: What is your self battery level after practicing?

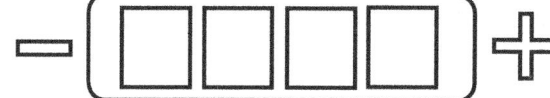

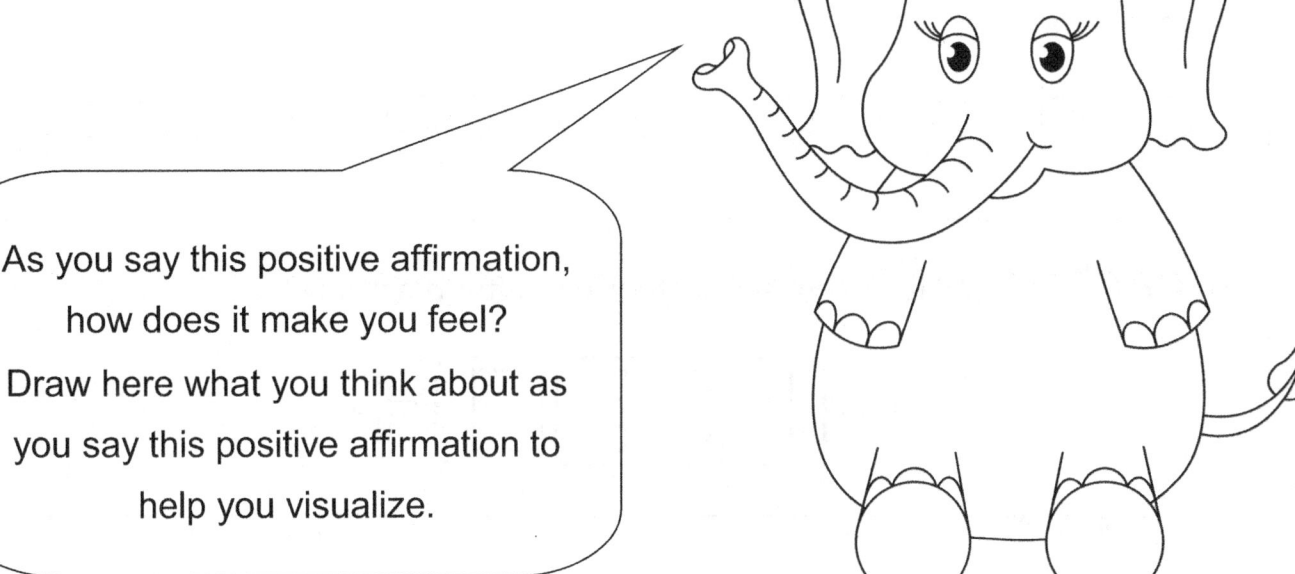

I am wise

Self Assessment: What is your self battery level before practicing?

Empowerment Pose: Superstar Pose
Stand in this empowerment pose for two minutes while repeating this affirmation.

Intentional Emotion: Write the emotion(s) you want to bring into the exercise in this space: _____

Scribe: Write affirmation in this space: _____

Repeat Affirmation Aloud: Use this space to tally how many times you repeat the affirmation:

○○○○○○○○○○○○○○○○○○○○○○○○○○

Reflection: What is your self battery level after practicing?

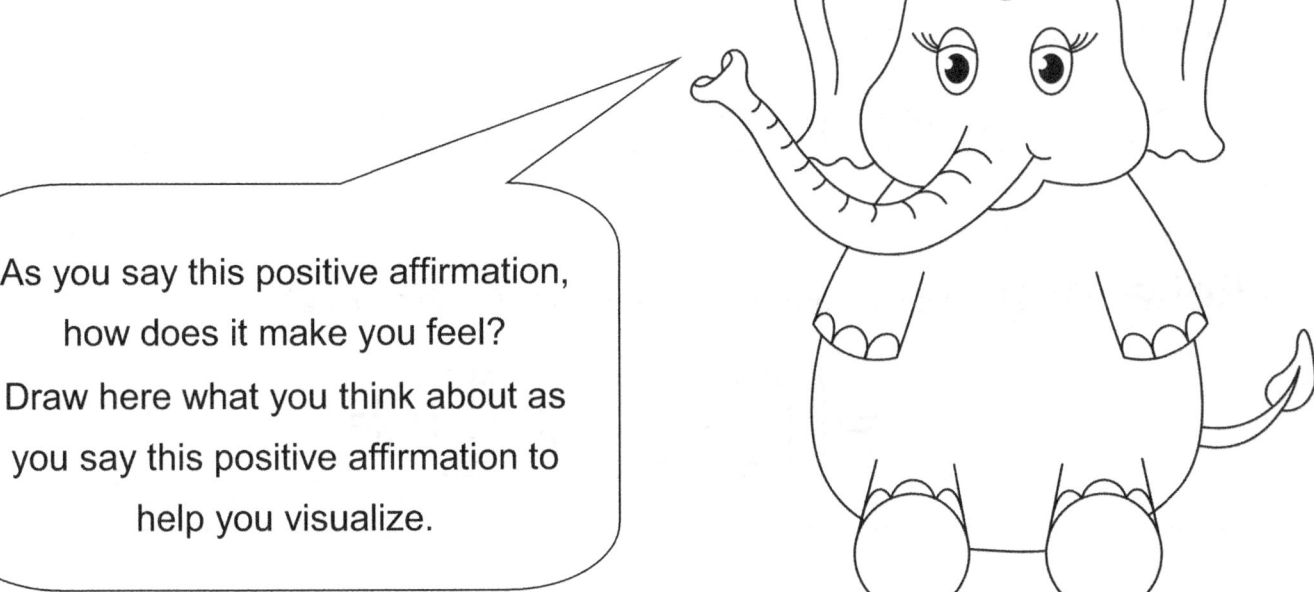

I am strong

Self Assessment: What is your self battery level before practicing?

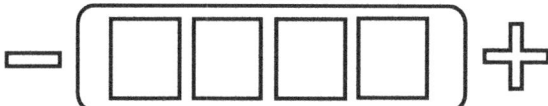

Empowerment Pose: Strength Pose
Stand in this empowerment pose for two minutes while repeating this affirmation.

Intentional Emotion: Write the emotion(s) you want to bring into the exercise in this space: _____
_____

Scribe: Write affirmation in this space: _____
_____

Repeat Affirmation Aloud: Use this space to tally how many times you repeat the affirmation:

○○○○○○○○○○○○○○○○○○○○○○

Reflection: What is your self battery level after practicing?

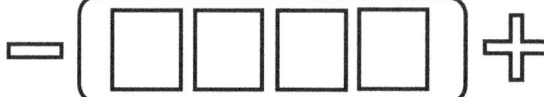

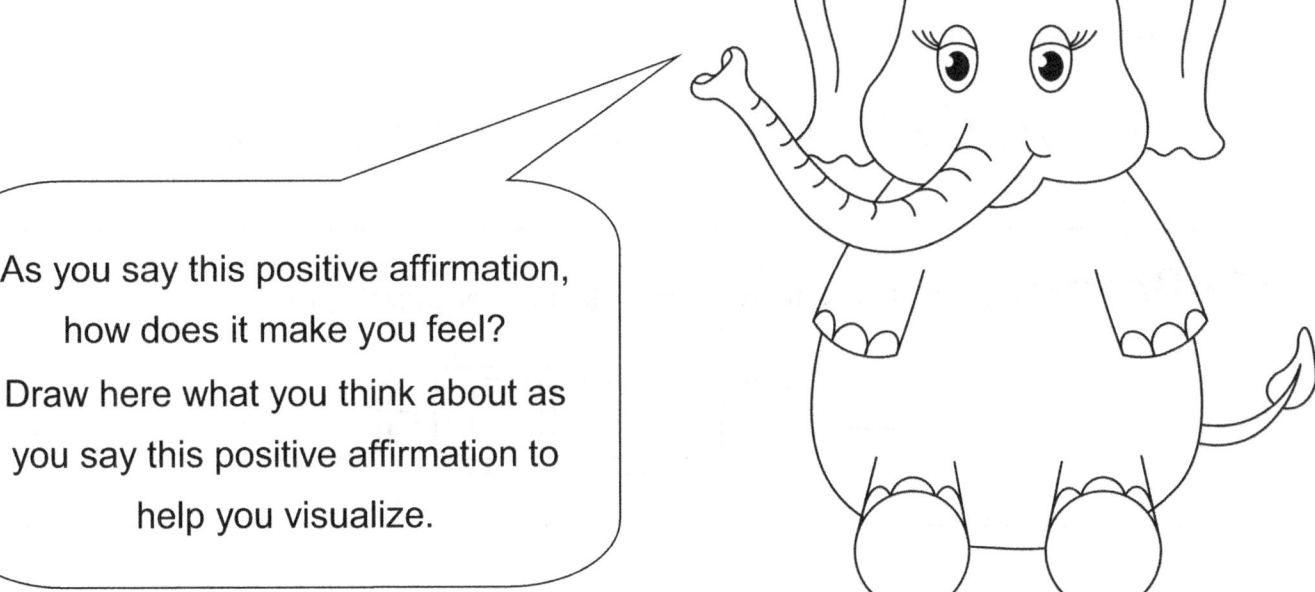

I am capable

Self Assessment: What is your self battery level before practicing?

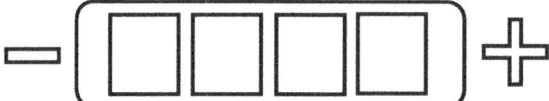

Empowerment Pose: **Victory Pose**
Stand in this empowerment pose for two minutes while repeating this affirmation.

Intentional Emotion: Write the emotion(s) you want to bring into the exercise in this space: _____

_____

Scribe: Write affirmation in this space: _____

_____

Repeat Affirmation Aloud: Use this space to tally how many times you repeat the affirmation:

○○○○○○○○○○○○○○○○○○○○○

Reflection: What is your self battery level after practicing?

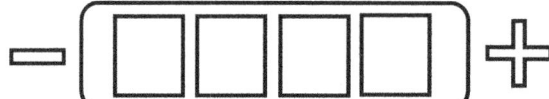

Visualization helps to deepen positive affirmations. Helping you step into the best you that you can be! Can you draw out your visualization below?

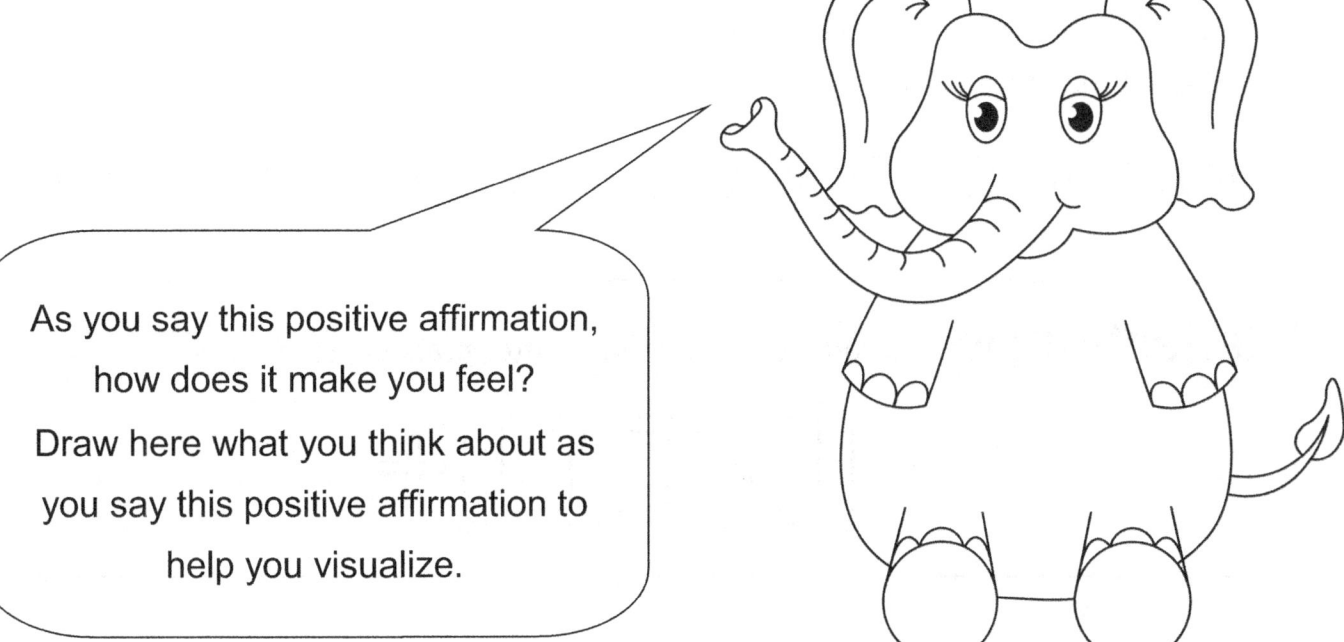

As you say this positive affirmation, how does it make you feel? Draw here what you think about as you say this positive affirmation to help you visualize.

I am worthy

Self Assessment: What is your self battery level before practicing?

− [ ][ ][ ][ ] +

Empowerment Pose: Confident Pose
Stand in this empowerment pose for two minutes while repeating this affirmation.

Intentional Emotion: Write the emotion(s) you want to bring into the exercise in this space: _____
_____

Scribe: Write affirmation in this space: _____
_____

Repeat Affirmation Aloud: Use this space to tally how many times you repeat the affirmation:

○○○○○○○○○○○○○○○○○○○○○○○○○

Reflection: What is your self battery level after practicing?

− [ ][ ][ ][ ] +

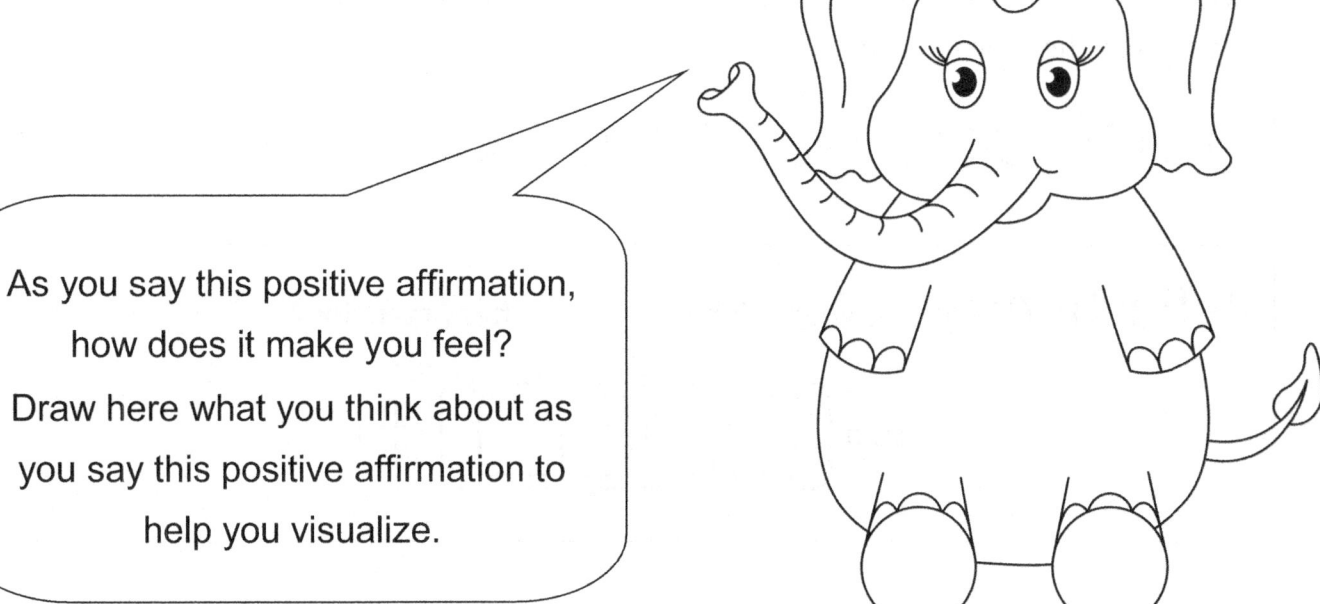

I am enough

Self Assessment: What is your self battery level before practicing?

− ▢▢▢▢ +

Empowerment Pose: Worthy Pose
Stand in this empowerment pose for two minutes while repeating this affirmation.

Intentional Emotion: Write the emotion(s) you want to bring into the exercise in this space: _____
_____

Scribe: Write affirmation in this space: _____
_____

Repeat Affirmation Aloud: Use this space to tally how many times you repeat the affirmation:

○○○○○○○○○○○○○○○○○○○○○○

Reflection: What is your self battery level after practicing?

− ▢▢▢▢ +

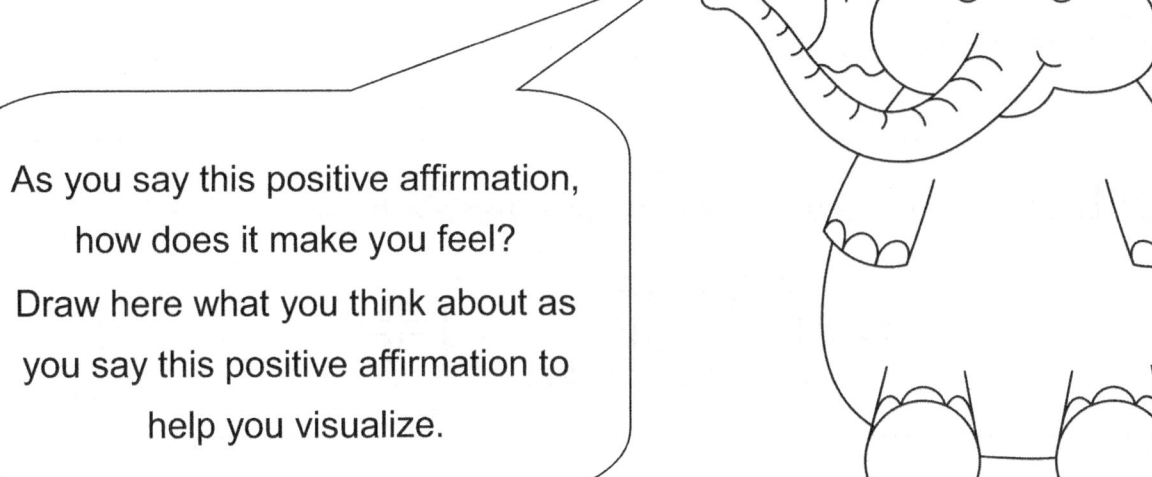

I am heard

Self Assessment: What is your self battery level before practicing?

— ▢▢▢▢ +

Empowerment Pose: Prosper Pose
Stand in this empowerment pose for two minutes while repeating this affirmation.

Intentional Emotion: Write the emotion(s) you want to bring into the exercise in this space: _____
_____

Scribe: Write affirmation in this space: _____
_____

Repeat Affirmation Aloud: Use this space to tally how many times you repeat the affirmation:

○○○○○○○○○○○○○○○○○○○○○○

Reflection: What is your self battery level after practicing?

— ▢▢▢▢ +

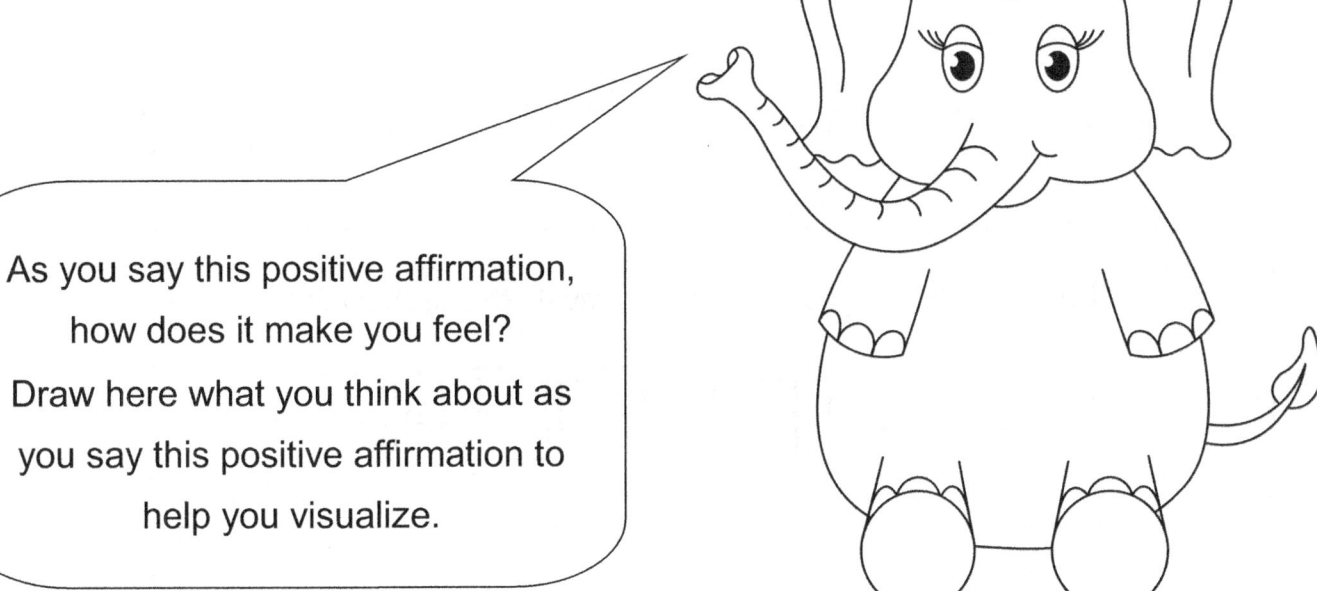

I am balanced

Self Assessment: What is your self battery level before practicing?

Empowerment Pose: Victory Pose
Stand in this empowerment pose for two minutes while repeating this affirmation.

Intentional Emotion: Write the emotion(s) you want to bring into the exercise in this space: _____

Scribe: Write affirmation in this space: _____

Repeat Affirmation Aloud: Use this space to tally how many times you repeat the affirmation:

○○○○○○○○○○○○○○○○○○○○○○○○

Reflection: What is your self battery level after practicing?

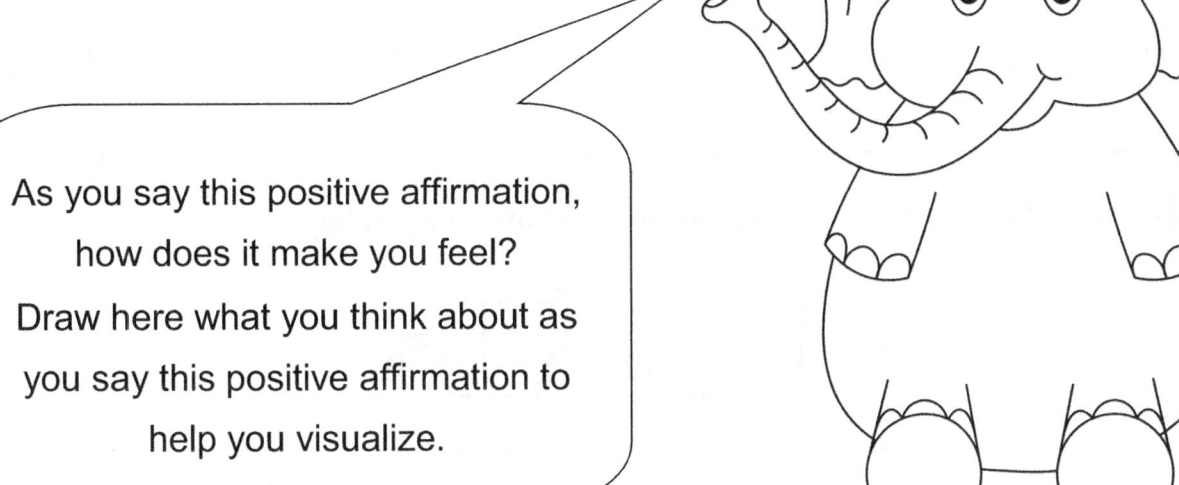

I am focused

Self Assessment: What is your self battery level before practicing?

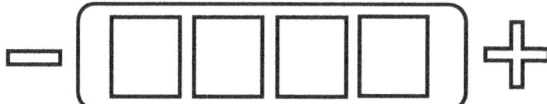

Empowerment Pose: Warrior Pose
Stand in this empowerment pose for two minutes while repeating this affirmation.

Intentional Emotion: Write the emotion(s) you want to bring into the exercise in this space: _____
_____

Scribe: Write affirmation in this space: _____
_____

Repeat Affirmation Aloud: Use this space to tally how many times you repeat the affirmation:

○○○○○○○○○○○○○○○○○○○○

Reflection: What is your self battery level after practicing?

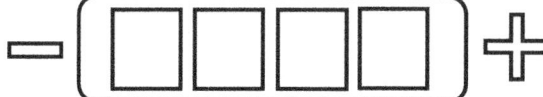

I am focused

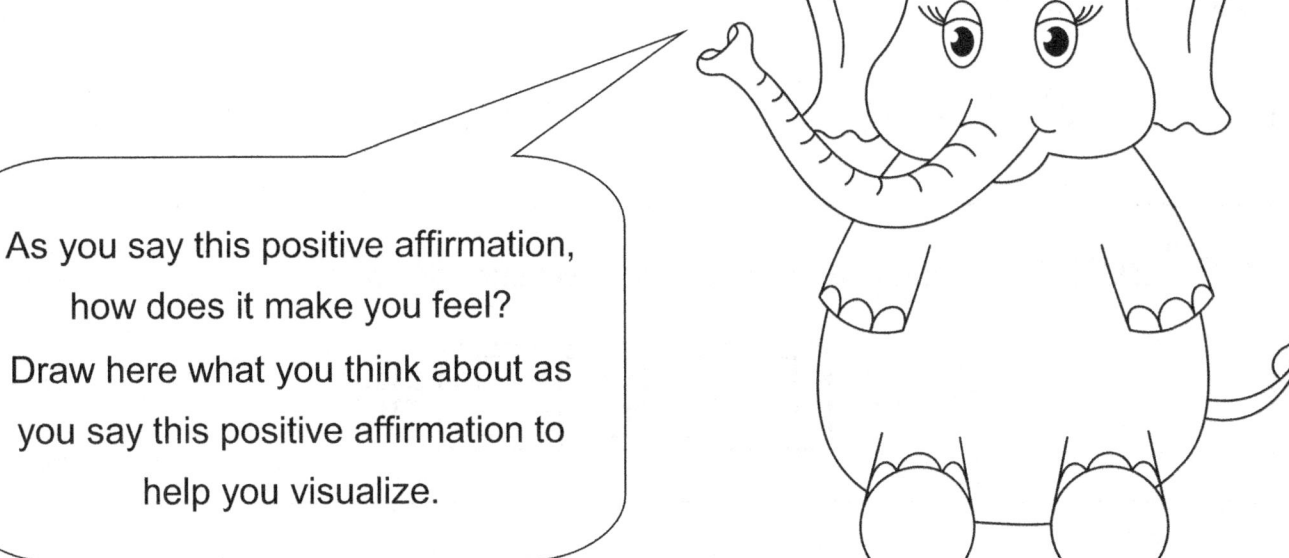

I am positive

Self Assessment: What is your self battery level before practicing?

− ▢▢▢▢ +

Empowerment Pose: Celebration Pose
Stand in this empowerment pose for two minutes while repeating this affirmation.

Intentional Emotion: Write the emotion(s) you want to bring into the exercise in this space: _____
_____

Scribe: Write affirmation in this space: _____
_____

Repeat Affirmation Aloud: Use this space to tally how many times you repeat the affirmation:

○○○○○○○○○○○○○○○○○○○○○○○○

Reflection: What is your self battery level after practicing?

− ▢▢▢▢ +

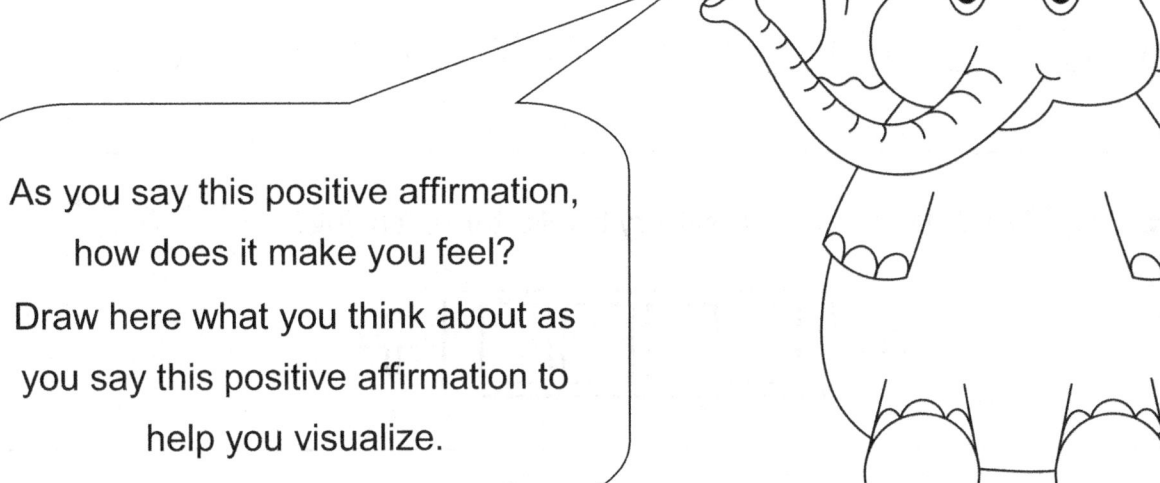

I am generous

Self Assessment: What is your self battery level before practicing?

— [☐ ☐ ☐ ☐] +

Empowerment Pose: Abundant Pose
Stand in this empowerment pose for two minutes while repeating this affirmation.

Intentional Emotion: Write the emotion(s) you want to bring into the exercise in this space: _____
_____

Scribe: Write affirmation in this space: _____
_____

Repeat Affirmation Aloud: Use this space to tally how many times you repeat the affirmation:

○○○○○○○○○○○○○○○○○○○○○○○○○

Reflection: What is your self battery level after practicing?

— [☐ ☐ ☐ ☐] +

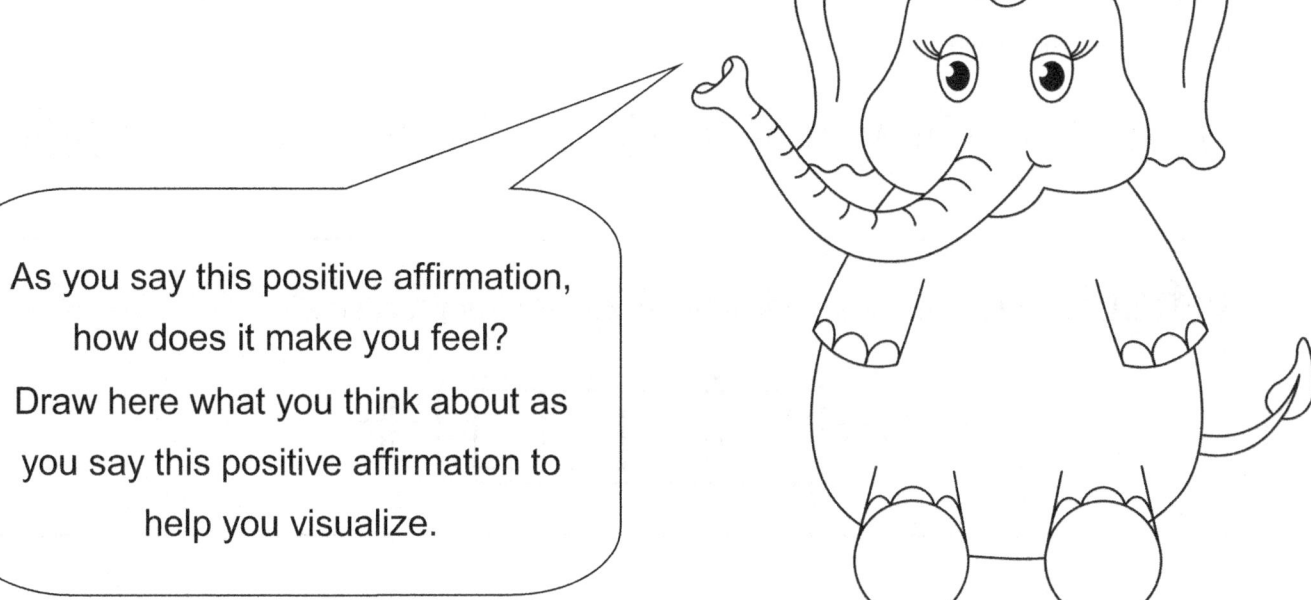

I am secure

Self Assessment: What is your self battery level before practicing?

— ▢▢▢▢ +

Empowerment Pose: Embrace Pose
Stand in this empowerment pose for two minutes while repeating this affirmation.

Intentional Emotion: Write the emotion(s) you want to bring into the exercise in this space: _____
_____

Scribe: Write affirmation in this space: _____
_____

Repeat Affirmation Aloud: Use this space to tally how many times you repeat the affirmation:

○○○○○○○○○○○○○○○○○○○○○○○

Reflection: What is your self battery level after practicing?

— ▢▢▢▢ +

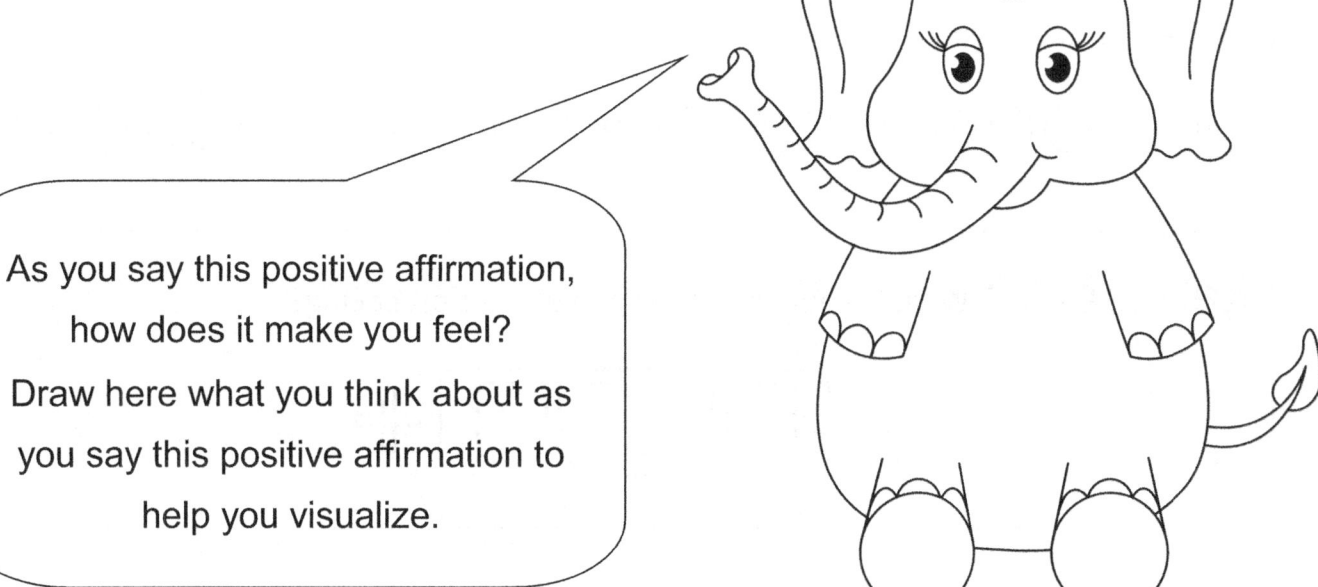

I am grateful

Self Assessment: What is your self battery level before practicing?

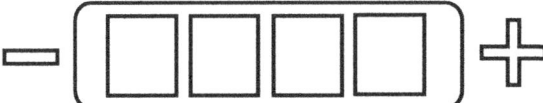

Empowerment Pose: Compassion Pose
Stand in this empowerment pose for two minutes while repeating this affirmation.

Intentional Emotion: Write the emotion(s) you want to bring into the exercise in this space: _____

_____

Scribe: Write affirmation in this space: _____

_____

Repeat Affirmation Aloud: Use this space to tally how many times you repeat the affirmation:

○○○○○○○○○○○○○○○○○○○○○○○○

Reflection: What is your self battery level after practicing?

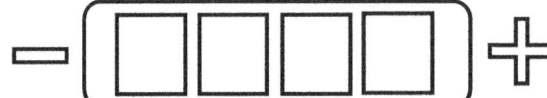

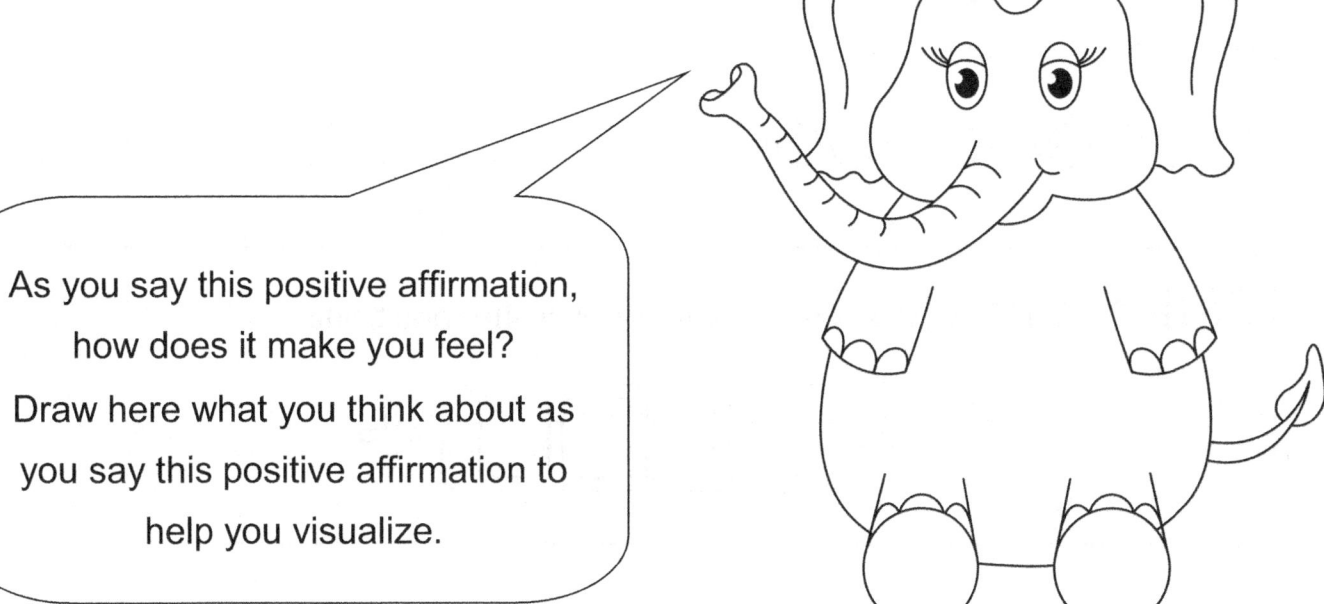

I am confident

Self Assessment: What is your self battery level before practicing?

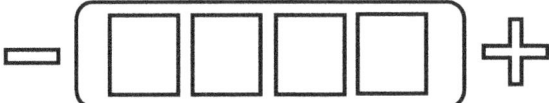

Empowerment Pose: **Leader Pose**
Stand in this empowerment pose for two minutes while repeating this affirmation.

Intentional Emotion: Write the emotion(s) you want to bring into the exercise in this space: _____

_____

Scribe: Write affirmation in this space: _____

_____

Repeat Affirmation Aloud: Use this space to tally how many times you repeat the affirmation:

○○○○○○○○○○○○○○○○○○○○○○

Reflection: What is your self battery level after practicing?

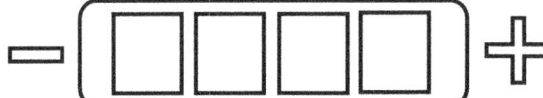

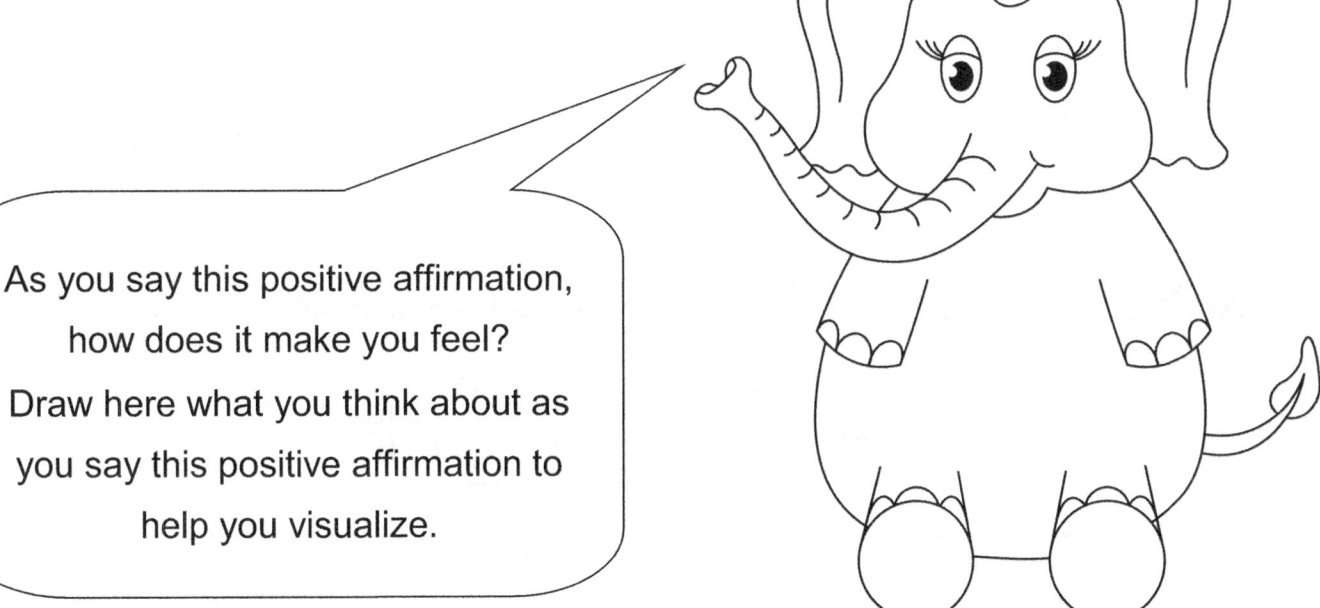

I am courageous

Self Assessment: What is your self battery level before practicing?

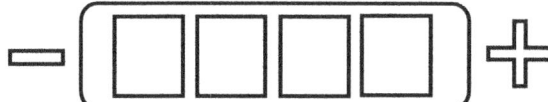

Empowerment Pose: Warrior Pose
Stand in this empowerment pose for two minutes while repeating this affirmation.

Intentional Emotion: Write the emotion(s) you want to bring into the exercise in this space: _____
_____

Scribe: Write affirmation in this space: _____
_____

Repeat Affirmation Aloud: Use this space to tally how many times you repeat the affirmation:

○○○○○○○○○○○○○○○○○○○○○○○○

Reflection: What is your self battery level after practicing?

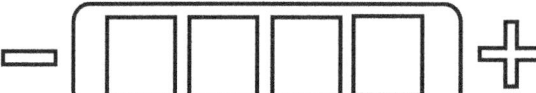

As you say this positive affirmation, how does it make you feel? Draw here what you think about as you say this positive affirmation to help you visualize.

I am Powerful

Self Assessment: What is your self battery level before practicing?

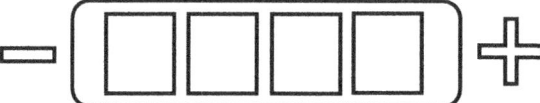

Empowerment Pose: Strength Pose
Stand in this empowerment pose for two minutes while repeating this affirmation.

Intentional Emotion: Write the emotion(s) you want to bring into the exercise in this space: _____
_____

Scribe: Write affirmation in this space: _____
_____

Repeat Affirmation Aloud: Use this space to tally how many times you repeat the affirmation:

○○○○○○○○○○○○○○○○○○○○○

Reflection: What is your self battery level after practicing?

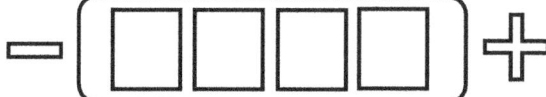

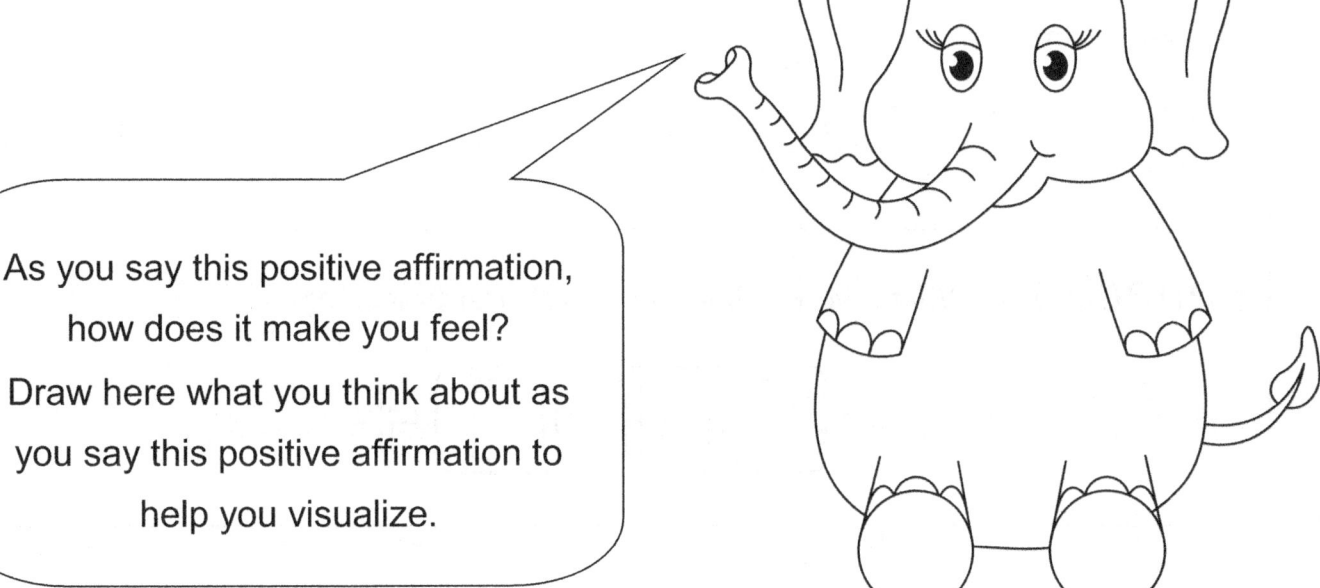

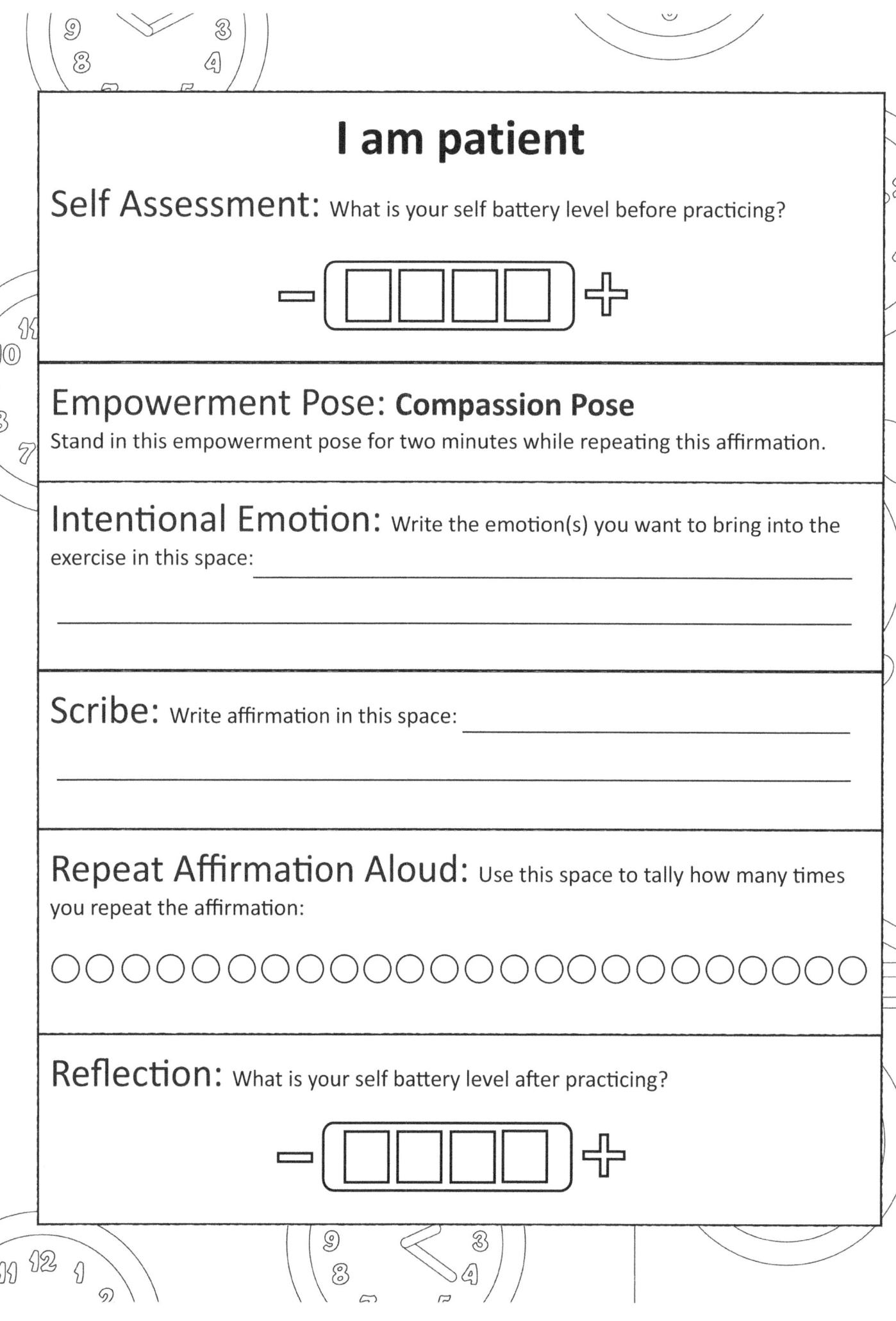

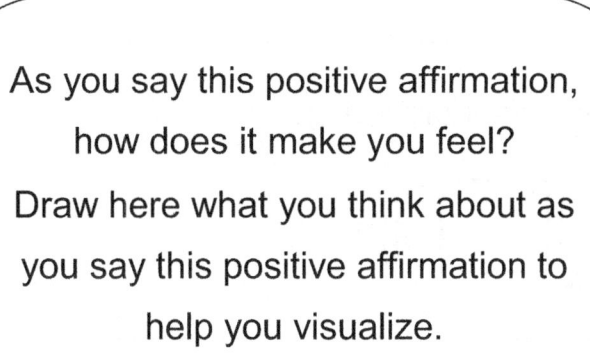

I am creative

Self Assessment: What is your self battery level before practicing?

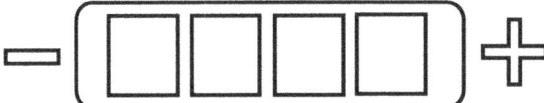

Empowerment Pose: Worthy Pose
Stand in this empowerment pose for two minutes while repeating this affirmation.

Intentional Emotion: Write the emotion(s) you want to bring into the exercise in this space: _____
_____

Scribe: Write affirmation in this space: _____
_____

Repeat Affirmation Aloud: Use this space to tally how many times you repeat the affirmation:

○○○○○○○○○○○○○○○○○○○○○○○○○

Reflection: What is your self battery level after practicing?

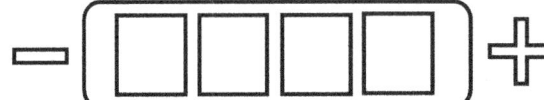

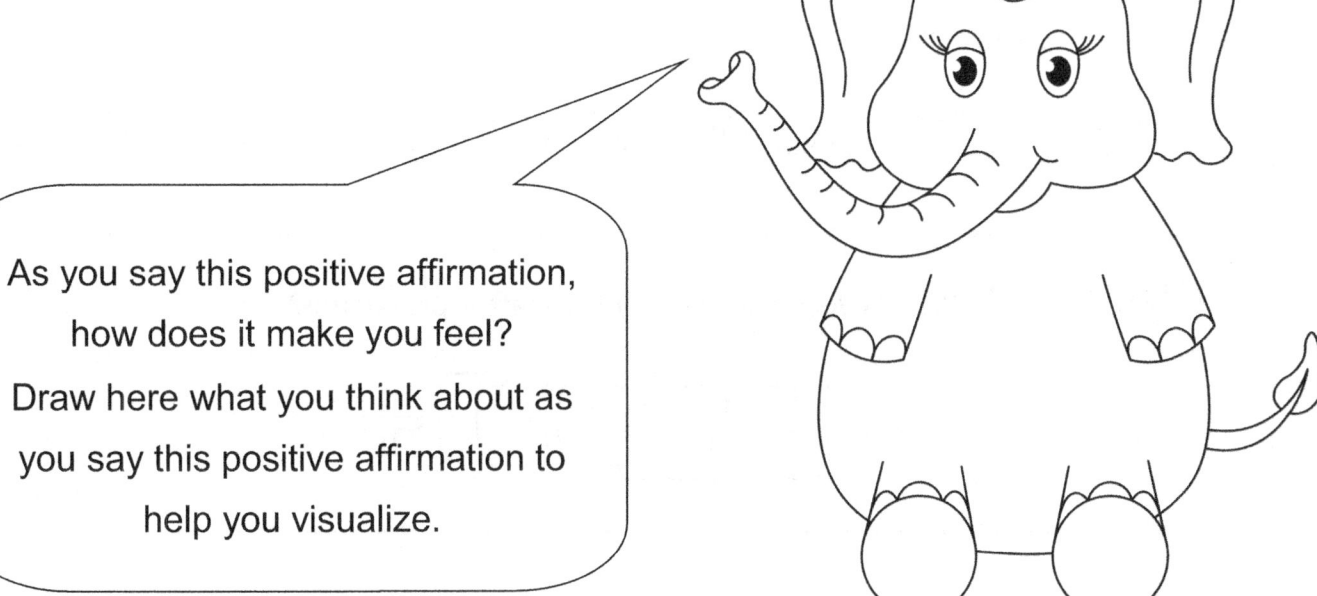

I am talented

Self Assessment: What is your self battery level before practicing?

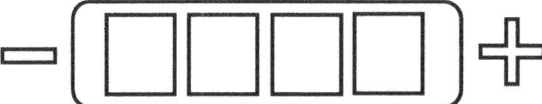

Empowerment Pose: Superstar Pose
Stand in this empowerment pose for two minutes while repeating this affirmation.

Intentional Emotion: Write the emotion(s) you want to bring into the exercise in this space: _____
_____

Scribe: Write affirmation in this space: _____
_____

Repeat Affirmation Aloud: Use this space to tally how many times you repeat the affirmation:

○○○○○○○○○○○○○○○○○○○○○○

Reflection: What is your self battery level after practicing?

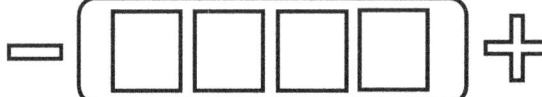

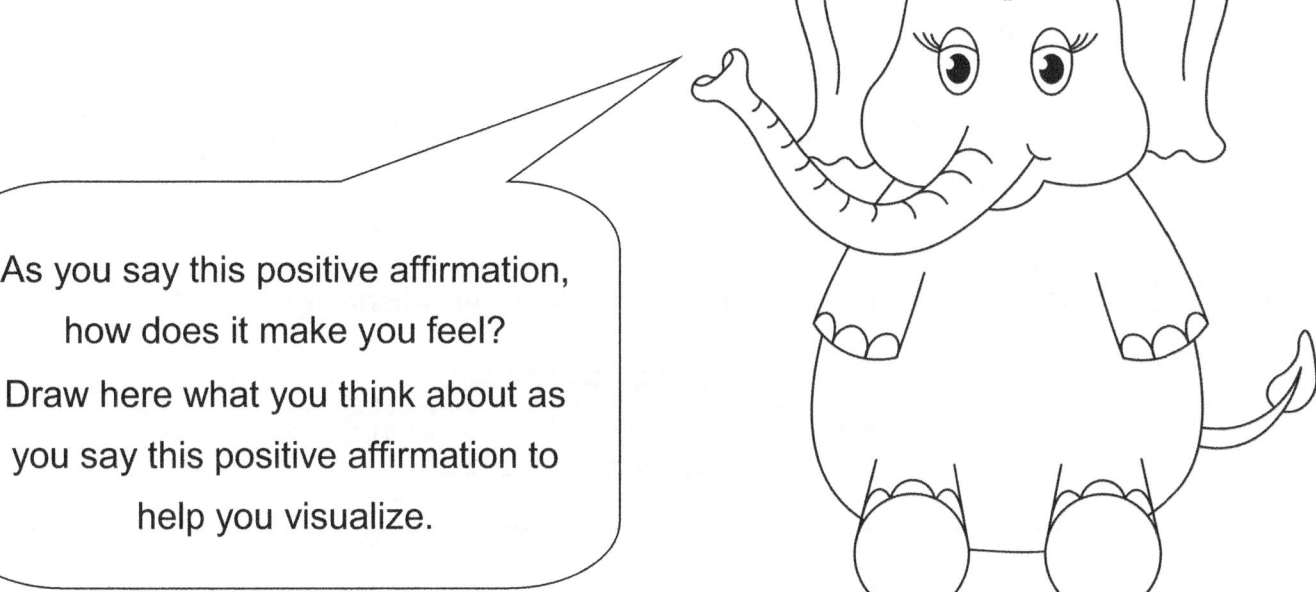

I am intelligent

Self Assessment: What is your self battery level before practicing?

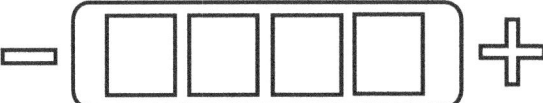

Empowerment Pose: Accomplished Pose
Stand in this empowerment pose for two minutes while repeating this affirmation.

Intentional Emotion: Write the emotion(s) you want to bring into the exercise in this space: _____

_____

Scribe: Write affirmation in this space: _____

_____

Repeat Affirmation Aloud: Use this space to tally how many times you repeat the affirmation:

○○○○○○○○○○○○○○○○○○○○○○○○

Reflection: What is your self battery level after practicing?

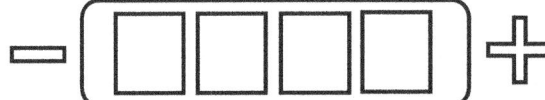

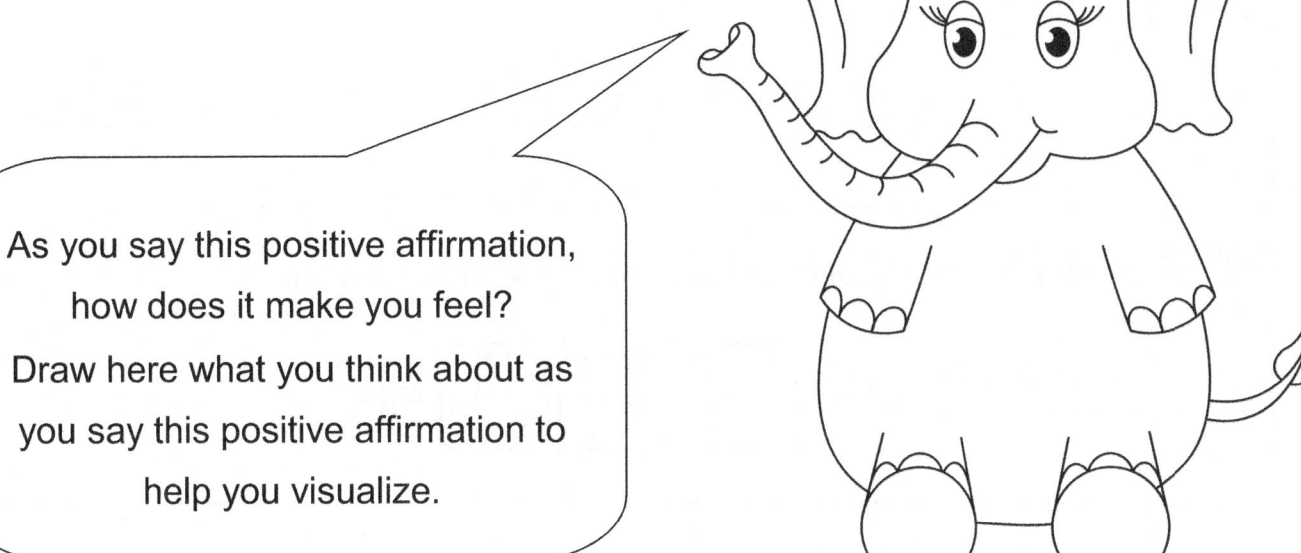

I am free

Self Assessment: What is your self battery level before practicing?

− ☐☐☐☐ +

Empowerment Pose: Celebration Pose
Stand in this empowerment pose for two minutes while repeating this affirmation.

Intentional Emotion: Write the emotion(s) you want to bring into the exercise in this space: _____
_____

Scribe: Write affirmation in this space: _____
_____

Repeat Affirmation Aloud: Use this space to tally how many times you repeat the affirmation:

○○○○○○○○○○○○○○○○○○○○○○○○○

Reflection: What is your self battery level after practicing?

− ☐☐☐☐ +

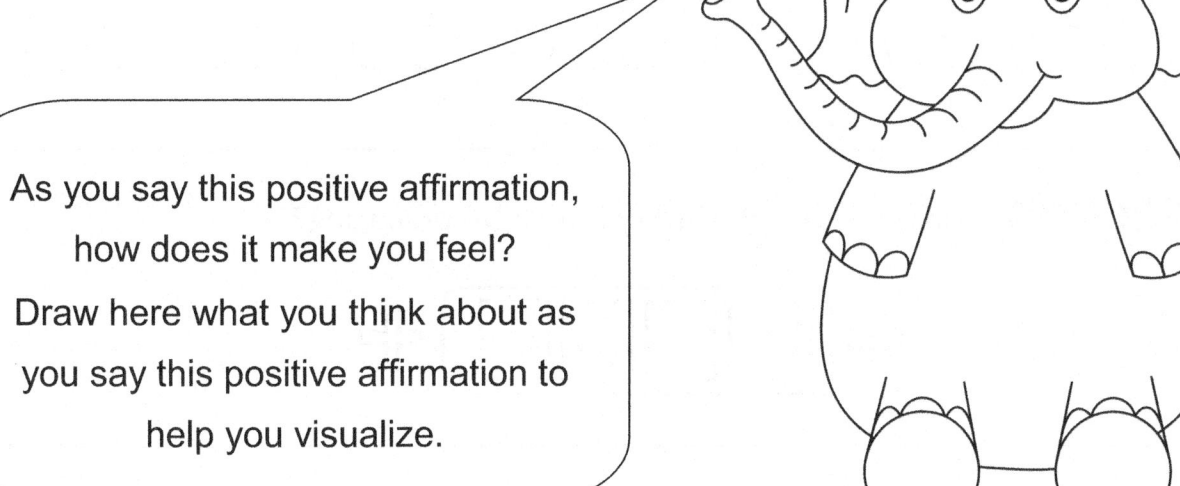

As you say this positive affirmation, how does it make you feel? Draw here what you think about as you say this positive affirmation to help you visualize.

I am grounded

Self Assessment: What is your self battery level before practicing?

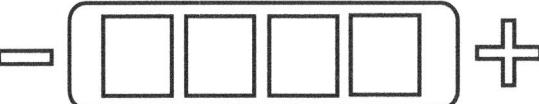

Empowerment Pose: Abundant Pose
Stand in this empowerment pose for two minutes while repeating this affirmation.

Intentional Emotion: Write the emotion(s) you want to bring into the exercise in this space: _____
_____

Scribe: Write affirmation in this space: _____
_____

Repeat Affirmation Aloud: Use this space to tally how many times you repeat the affirmation:

○○○○○○○○○○○○○○○○○○○○○○○

Reflection: What is your self battery level after practicing?

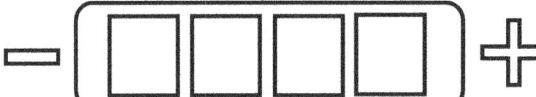

I am grounded

Visualization helps to deepen positive affirmations. Helping you step into the best you that you can be! Can you draw out your visualization below?

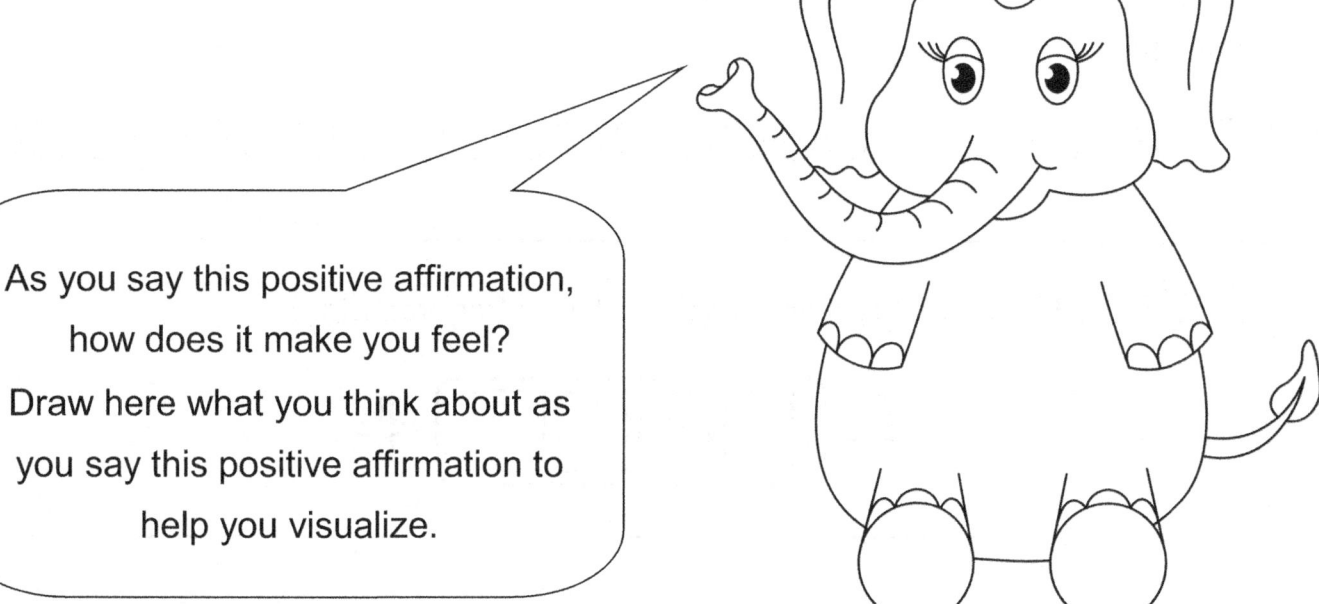

As you say this positive affirmation, how does it make you feel? Draw here what you think about as you say this positive affirmation to help you visualize.

I am peaceful

Self Assessment: What is your self battery level before practicing?

Empowerment Pose: Grounded Pose
Stand in this empowerment pose for two minutes while repeating this affirmation.

Intentional Emotion: Write the emotion(s) you want to bring into the exercise in this space: _____
_____

Scribe: Write affirmation in this space: _____
_____

Repeat Affirmation Aloud: Use this space to tally how many times you repeat the affirmation:

○○○○○○○○○○○○○○○○○○○○○○○

Reflection: What is your self battery level after practicing?

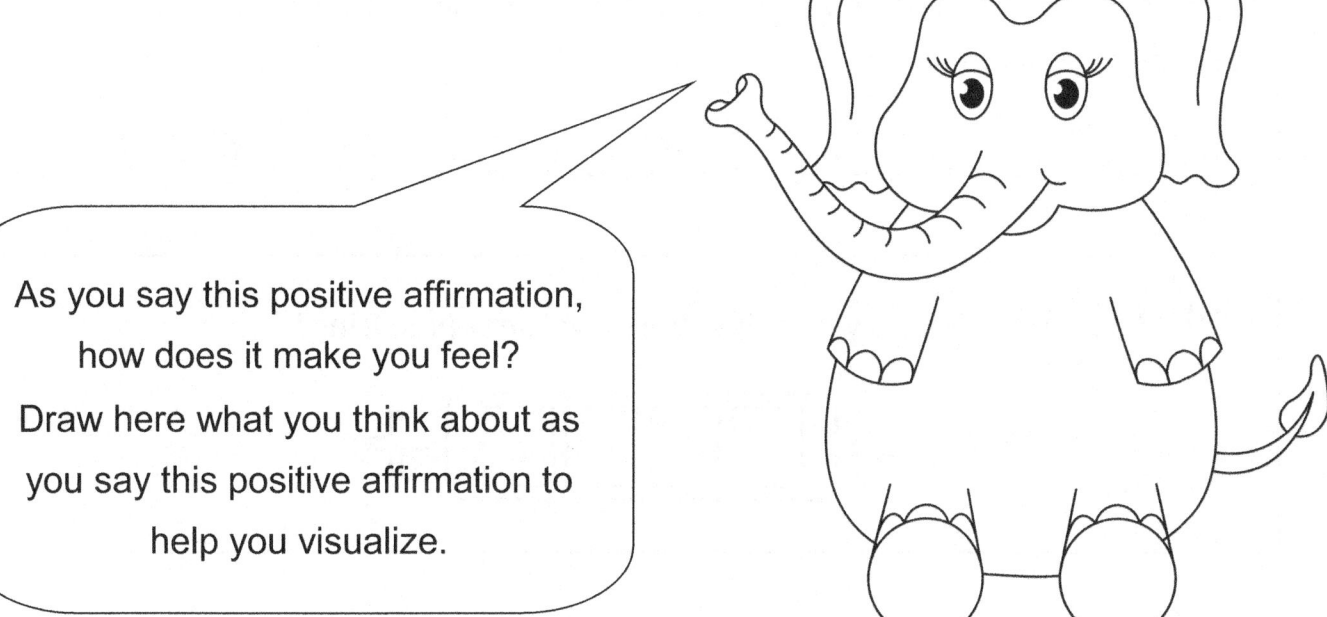

I am protected

Self Assessment: What is your self battery level before practicing?

Empowerment Pose: Embrace Pose
Stand in this empowerment pose for two minutes while repeating this affirmation.

Intentional Emotion: Write the emotion(s) you want to bring into the exercise in this space: _____

_____

Scribe: Write affirmation in this space: _____

_____

Repeat Affirmation Aloud: Use this space to tally how many times you repeat the affirmation:

◯◯◯◯◯◯◯◯◯◯◯◯◯◯◯◯◯◯◯◯

Reflection: What is your self battery level after practicing?

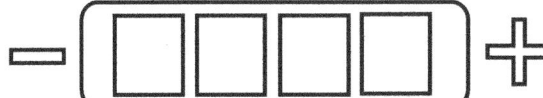

Visualization helps to deepen positive affirmations. Helping you step into the best you that you can be! Can you draw out your visualization below?

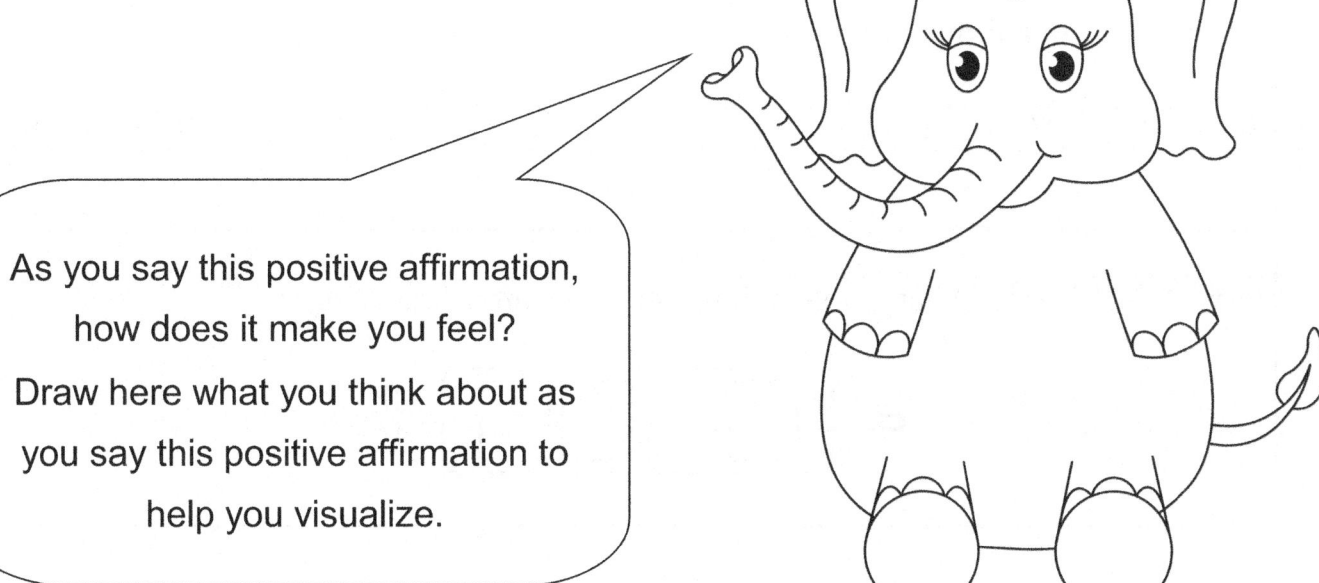

I am brave

Self Assessment: What is your self battery level before practicing?

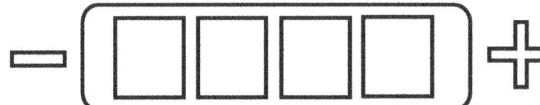

Empowerment Pose: Courageous Pose
Stand in this empowerment pose for two minutes while repeating this affirmation.

Intentional Emotion: Write the emotion(s) you want to bring into the exercise in this space: _____

_____

Scribe: Write affirmation in this space: _____

_____

Repeat Affirmation Aloud: Use this space to tally how many times you repeat the affirmation:

○○○○○○○○○○○○○○○○○○○○○○

Reflection: What is your self battery level after practicing?

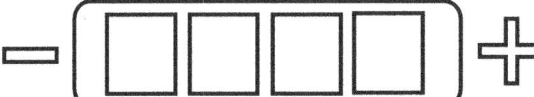

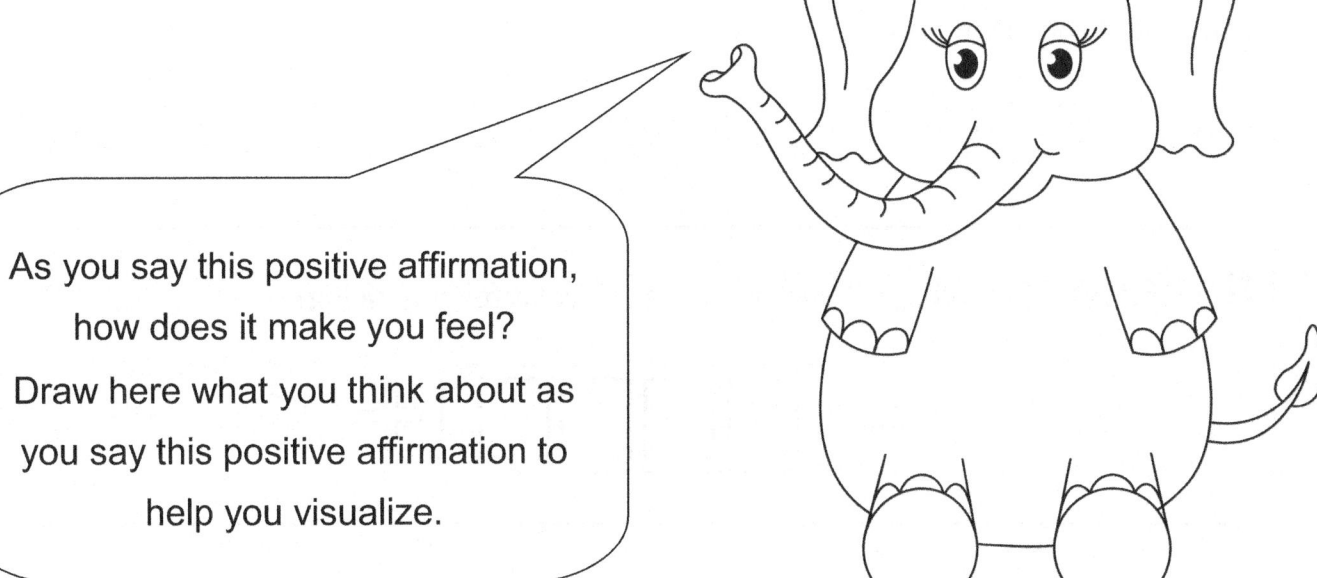

I am unique

Self Assessment: What is your self battery level before practicing?

− ▢▢▢▢ +

Empowerment Pose: Superhero Pose
Stand in this empowerment pose for two minutes while repeating this affirmation.

Intentional Emotion: Write the emotion(s) you want to bring into the exercise in this space: _____
_____

Scribe: Write affirmation in this space: _____
_____

Repeat Affirmation Aloud: Use this space to tally how many times you repeat the affirmation:

○○○○○○○○○○○○○○○○○○○○○○○○○

Reflection: What is your self battery level after practicing?

− ▢▢▢▢ +

As you say this positive affirmation, how does it make you feel? Draw here what you think about as you say this positive affirmation to help you visualize.

I am unstoppable

Self Assessment: What is your self battery level before practicing?

Empowerment Pose: Transcendent Pose
Stand in this empowerment pose for two minutes while repeating this affirmation.

Intentional Emotion: Write the emotion(s) you want to bring into the exercise in this space: _____
_____

Scribe: Write affirmation in this space: _____
_____

Repeat Affirmation Aloud: Use this space to tally how many times you repeat the affirmation:

○○○○○○○○○○○○○○○○○○○○○○

Reflection: What is your self battery level after practicing?

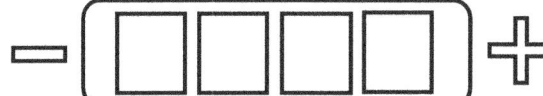

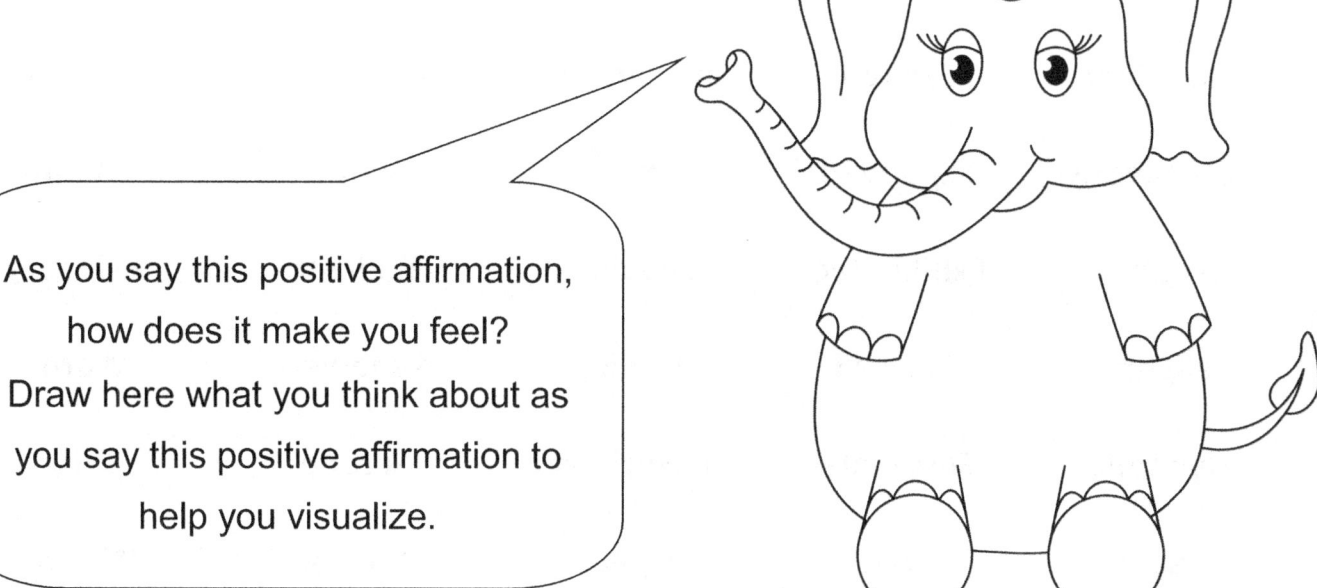

Create Your Own Positive Affirmations

1. Notice a negative thought about yourself and write down the positive opposite that counteracts that belief.

2. Make it short.

3. Use present tense.

4. Create your affirmation as an expression of being grateful for already having and being what you want.

5. Make an affirmation that you believe. If it's hard to believe then start it with, "I am willing to believe I could …." or " … is improving every day" or "I am open to…"

To help you get started below are some positive words you can use in your affirmations:

Amazed	Empowered	Happy	Optimistic	Thankful
Appreciated	Energetic	Harmonious	Passionate	Understanding
Appreciative	Enthusiastic	Inspired	Positive	Unlimited
Confident	Excited	Invigorated	Powerful	Uplifted
Courageous	Expanded	Joyful	Proud	Vibrant
Creative	Exhilarated	Lovable	Radiant	Visionary
Delighted	Focused	Loving	Renewed	Warm
Dynamic	Fortunate	Luxurious	Serene	Wise
Eager	Free	Open	Strong	Worthy

Create Your Own Positive Affirmations

_____

_____

_____

_____

_____

_____

Gratitude Journal

These pages are for you to have a space to write or draw what you are grateful for. Having gratitude helps us look at the positive in our lives.

_____

_____

_____

Disclaimer

You are solely responsible for the way that this information is perceived and utilized and do so at your own risk. The exercise information provided is of a general nature and can not be substituted for the advice provided by a medical doctor or certified health practitioner. This information is designed for educational purposes only and must not be construed as medical advice or professional service, and not for diagnosis, prescription or treatment of any health disorders. The author of this book is not liable or responsible to any person for any errors contained in this information, or for any special, incidental, or consequential injury caused or alleged to be caused direction or indirectly by the information contained in this book. This agreement is governed by CA law and any disputes shall be resolved in Palm Desert, CA.

About Coping In Color Series

We hope you enjoyed your In Color experience!
Visit www.calmandcolorful.com to:

Embrace your inner Calm & Colorful Mama: For coping tools, travel tips, jokes, and more join our *free* Newsletter.

Connect with us: Please share with us about your coping skills journey. Tag us (@calmandcolorful) on your post of you practicing the exercises or reading the book. Describe your journey on our social media pages (Facebook, Instagram, and TikTok)

Read or write a review: Read what others have to say about our books or post your own review on Amazon or email us (reviews@calmandcolorful.com) a review. We would love to hear from you!

Check out our other books: Check out our other books in the In Color series teaching breathing, yoga, affirmations, empowerment poses, mudras, emotional freedom technique, mindfulness and much more!

FREE Color & Cope session: Email me to set up a free 30 minute virtual session where you (or your child) picks out your favorite exercise and we color and practice the coping skill together.

With love & gratitiude,
Jessica Brittani

www.calmandcolorful.com
books@calmandcolorful.com
www.Instagram.com/calmandcolorful
www.facebook.com/groups/calmandcolorfulmama/
www.tiktok.com/@calmandcolorful
www.amazon.com/stores/author/B08LB9KNQX

Made in the USA
Monee, IL
17 April 2024

56870613R10077